THE LIFESPAN OF CATS

THE LIFESPAN OF CATS

LEONARD CRIMSON

CONTENTS

1 Introduction — 1

2 Understanding Feline Anatomy and Physiology — 3

3 Nutritional Requirements for Cats — 5

4 Common Feline Health Issues and Diseases — 7

5 Preventive Care for Cats — 9

6 Vaccinations and Parasite Control — 11

7 Dental Health in Cats — 13

8 Senior Cat Care — 15

9 Behavioral and Environmental Enrichment — 17

10 Emergency Care and First Aid for Cats — 19

11 Breeding and Reproduction in Cats — 21

12 Feline Genetics and Breed-Specific Health Concerns — 23

13 Alternative and Complementary Therapies for Cats — 25

14 The Role of Exercise and Play in Feline Health — 27

15 Caring for Kittens — 29

16 Grooming and Hygiene for Cats — 31

17 Understanding Cat Communication and Body Language
33

18 The Importance of Spaying and Neutering   35

19 Traveling with Cats: Tips for a Stress-Free Journe   37

20 Caring for Multiple Cats in a Household   39

21 Cats in Different Life Stages: Kitten, Adult, and   41

22 Legal and Ethical Considerations in Feline Health   43

23 Cultural and Historical Perspectives on Cats   45

24 The Future of Feline Health: Advances in Veterinar   47

25 Conclusion and Key Takeaways   49

CHAPTER 1

Introduction

Cats are popular pets that can live for fifteen years or more. Knowing as well as you can the variables that determine the lifespan of a cat is a key first step toward making choices regarding your pet that will contribute to optimal health and well-being. In this guide, we will provide an overview of the lifespan of cats and review the most crucial approaches to practicing good healthcare for cats of all ages and life stages.

Certainly, no one knows just when their cat will die, but when you bring a pet into your home, you are effectively welcoming it into your family. If you take your cat to the veterinarian, observe a basic list of health and nourishment guidelines, and train yourself to be alert to the physical and behavioral clues of your cat's well-being, you will have the grounding needed to offer your pet the healthiest and happiest life it can potentially have. This guide will lead you through the most vital issues of feline health. Being prepared is key, particularly if you are considering sharing your life with a cat (or more than one cat).

In the following sections, we will provide the lifespans for the following categories of cats and advice on the best way to monitor their health: kittens, adults, seniors, cats with exceptional and/or additional healthcare concerns, and cats in different settings, such as indoor and outdoor environments. We will conclude with extra details about two circumstances that significantly impact the state of a cat's health: excessive shedding and obesity.

CHAPTER 2

Understanding Feline Anatomy and Physiology

It is essential to study the intricate relationship of feline anatomy and physiology at the dawn of the twenty-first century, as they serve as the foundation of feline health. Felines possess a number of characteristics reflective of their anatomy; such traits make them unique, and knowledge of these characteristics aids a veterinarian's understanding when treating sick or injured animals in the clinical setting. Physiology is the study of the living organisms' body processes, encompassing numerous systems that must function effectively in order to maintain life. The purpose of feline physiology is to identify the internal workings of the body and the processes that occur as a living organism performs simple, normal bodily functions or activities.

This chapter provides an in-depth view of the fundamental structure that is the feline anatomy, as well as the physiological systems (both individual and a group). Discussion of these systems is informative, helping one comprehend as the book progresses how various topics are interrelated. An understanding of feline anatomy and physiology is critical for comprehending feline health and illness, and is therefore discussed at the beginning of this text. This inclusion forms the foundation of the upcoming chapters and allows the study of the information that is to come, to be an understanding of particular aspects of health.

CHAPTER 3

Nutritional Requirements for Cats

The proper nutrition of cats is essential for maintaining their health and well-being throughout their life. Several nutrients are essential and necessary to ensure complete and balanced development, prevent disease, and prolong their life. In order to provide them with the correct nutrition, the dietary needs of cats of different ages and conditions need to be satisfied. Providing balanced diets will help your cat to remain strong, maintain healthy tissues and organs, and maintain a healthy immune system. Malnutrition can lead to obesity, underweight, dehydration, skeletal, visual, cardiac, renal and reproductive abnormalities, lead to serious disease, and may be associated with a shortened lifespan.

The following represent the five specific dietary guidelines: 1) Fresh water should always be available. 2) The amount of meals depends on the cat's life stage, size, and age. 3) A balanced diet at each stage of their life. Kittens who are still growing need twice as much protein and an additional 50 percent of essential nutrients as adults. 4) Choose food based on the recipes and ingredients your cat likes. 5) Overfeeding behavior is not good because cats do not usually eat more than is necessary. It is important to consider the energy and nutritional requirements at different stages of their life. A detailed explanation of the recent knowledge in the importance of specific nutrients and their requirement for overall health and during distinct life stages is described.

CHAPTER 4

Common Feline Health Issues and Diseases

Veterinary experts estimate that cats can experience anywhere from 34 to 250 ailments during their lifetime. While this comprehensive range undoubtedly includes rare conditions that affect only a small percentage of the feline population, it is also indicative of the diverse range of health issues that cats can face over their lifetime. This book includes a detailed examination of many of the most widespread conditions and diseases that cats may encounter during their lives, looking over the causes, symptoms, typical course, and treatment options for each ailment. As responsible caretakers, it is our duty to understand and be aware of the most prevalent health concerns that affect cats, as this will better enable us to recognize symptoms or signs of a problem, know when to act, and understand what our veterinarian recommends for prompt attention and care.

This is why this section in particular is crucial. It starts with cat health in a more general overview before discussing four sections on general conditions, external conditions, internal conditions, and viral and parasitic diseases. It goes over common diseases within those sections, bridging them with euthanasia and quality of life considerations. Hopefully this section will inspire cat owners to research each condition so that you'll be prepared should one of them befall their own feline friend. Nothing is more comforting in times of strife than to know that you have resources and tools at your disposal to overcome it.

CHAPTER 5

Preventive Care for Cats

Vet-recommended preventive care is a cornerstone of feline healthcare. A proactive, preventive approach involves not only regular check-ups, but also practices to prevent illness, maintain a healthy environment, and provide for a cat's quality of life. In "The Lifespan of Cats," we explain that disease may not particularly alter a cat's lifespan (life expectancy). Instead, negative influences on a cat's quality of life may lower that lifespan or might be practiced inappropriately or undervalued, decreasing a cat's lifespan. Preventive care is the basis of the proactive, progressive healthcare in which we should be active participants. These are the fundamental concepts and suggestions to prevent disease, illness, and hard times in our cat companions. Progress, optimize, take seriously, prioritize, and love your cat.

Quality-of-life events are made important and can become disease because of regular feline healthcare prophylactic disease concepts or because of progress in medical knowledge. Lifecycle approach, pasture (vaccinate). Perform regular feline healthcare by a proactive comprehensive veterinary physical exams may be unnecessary to receive vaccinations. Years 1-2. Limit environmental stress, environmental allergies, and geriatric changes. Onset FIV/FeLV test. Continue or switch to adult outdoor life. Twice a year monitor for

senior blood work including T3. Screen for and possible behavior issues. Inspect oral hygiene and begin adult oral hygiene plan. Shorten
vaccination interval (first 5-8 weeks) until 14 weeks or 3 vaccinations
are current.

CHAPTER 6

Vaccinations and Parasite Control

In the first 6-8 weeks of life, kittens are protected from infection with their mother's antibody-rich milk, provided soon after birth. However, the protection wears off soon after, so it is important that kittens are vaccinated young, with a repeat dose, or doses, roughly a month later. Neutering and microchipping often occur at the same time as the second kitten vaccination, although younger kittens can be neutered and microchipped at the same time of being desexed. Adult cats are generally considered to need vaccination boosters once every year based on various factors, including the types of vaccinations used.

Discuss this with your veterinarian who will be able to provide the most relevant information in your situation. Beyond kittens and their mothers, it is generally a case-by-case basis when it comes to vaccination in cats, and there may be particular reasons to vaccinate against some of the following diseases, depending on the animals involved and the risk factors they are exposed to. It is important to remember that vaccines are also important for the health of individual cats and have enormous benefits for the health of the general cat population also. Even if your cat is kept indoors or never exposed to other cats, it is still possible for infectious diseases to enter the home, for example via your hands, clothing or shoes, meaning the 'non risk-based' vaccinations (those recommended for all cats) may be justified for your pet. So while your pet may stay safe and happy in its own little world, if the common cat population in Australia were unvaccinated, there would definitely be an increased risk of disease for your pet just by virtue of the pets it may come into contact with. And potentially, the more unvaccinated cats around, the greater the risk.

CHAPTER 7

Dental Health in Cats

Cats commonly experience poor oral health throughout their lives, so it is essential to care for cats' teeth from a young age. Keep reading below for more information on caring for cats' teeth that can help maintain a healthy life for cats.

The cat's tooth consists of four main parts, namely the enamel, dentine, tooth root, and tooth crown. Around 20 adult teeth are located in the maxilla, while around 22 adult teeth are located in the mandible. Cats have carnivorous characteristics, so their canine teeth are quite long and pointed for tearing necks. In addition to the canine teeth, cats also have a number of premolars and molars, which are flat with a rough edge, to chew meat.

To care for the teeth of cats, you can entrust a veterinarian to perform a dental examination with X-rays. If there is tartar, the cat will be given tartar-cleaning powder with a special brush. In addition to getting professional dental care for cats, external action is also needed. You can do regular cleaning by providing a brush and toothpaste for cats. It is strongly discouraged to use toothpaste for humans because it could harm the cat's oral cavity. Generally, regular cat teeth care is needed to maintain good oral health. Cats are prone to various dental problems throughout their lives, primarily due to poor oral care. Dental problems that are commonly experienced by cats include tooth decay or dental caries, periodontal disease, Feline Odontoclastic Resorptive Lesions (FORL), and gingivitis. Most of these problems can be prevented by proper oral care for cats and regularly checking the oral cavity of the cat.

CHAPTER 8

Senior Cat Care

While senior cat care traditionally refers to cats aged 11 years or older, changes in overall genetics and veterinary care can see that age older, with many cats over the age of 10 still enjoying life's activities. Taking meticulous care of your senior cat means a bit more than the average annual or biannual check-ups at the veterinary office. Cats are considered geriatric at around 15 years old. When cats start to age, it's similar to when humans age: our bodies aren't as nimble, we may find it more difficult to keep at an optimal weight or it may be more difficult to carry out regular activities. Cats begin to find it hard to adapt their metabolism and the cell repair process may be affected. Around the age of 11 to 12, senior cats begin experiencing age-related issues earlier than cats, namely: arthritis, kidney and heart concerns, and lumps and bumps that are not as common in young cats. Older kitties may become grumpier, aggression or hiding due to painful illness may manifest, grooming behaviors and toileting behaviors may change.

Wellness But there are preventative measures in place to best alleviate those symptoms and, in many cases, adding time to the lives of cats. It is good senior care to take a full physical examination by a veterinarian at least once a year. Depending on the health status of your senior cat, blood work and urine testing are commonly performed (and sometimes other diagnostic tests such as x-rays or ultrasounds). Wellness testing is also carried out at least once a year. As cats are stoic animals and tend to hide any vulnerabilities or injuries, early detection and intervention for age-related problems are key. Many of the skin diseases, dental problems, and swelling which cats can face, and more, are known to veterinarians who are professional in treatment and categorical work. Supportive Care Many senior cats require supportive care to varying degrees in order to help maintain their vitality and comfort.

CHAPTER 9

Behavioral and Environmental Enrichment

Although cats possess many of the same neural substrates that govern socioemotional functions in humans and other mammals, breeding practices generally include intensive breeding and rearing of cats away from their mothers, and long-term housing in minimalistic living spaces without the opportunity to express natural behaviors may render traditional categories of abnormal behavior inapplicable to cats. Feline sociability and relations to the humans in their lives through both direct interactions and via the manipulation of the physically fostered environment need to be re-addressed. If they are to be of real-world relevance to cat carers, the different but highly prevalent behavioral challenges felines are faced with may need to be categorized in terms of time constraints and the emotional systems that may mediate the challenge. The purpose of environmental enrichment is to promote mental and physical stimulation, reducing stress and verbalizing natural behaviors as well as facilitating adaptation to the shelter and adoptive homes.

The goal of an enrichment plan is to enhance every one of the five principles as much as imaginable. Environmental enrichment is not just about ensuring satisfactory production behavior, but it is also about ensuring the welfare of those animals. Addressing environmental enrichment for domestic cats goes far beyond just placing a post to scratch on or a toy to play with in the cage. In order for the cats' behavior to improve forever, there must be a change in the way they are housed. If the effective programs and support are in place, environmental enrichment will help to address many of the behavior problems of domestic cats, as detailed in this paper.

CHAPTER 10

Emergency Care and First Aid for Cats

In our section on health concerns, we go in-depth on emergency care and first aid to ensure your feline is always safe and looked after. Cats are curious creatures, and their curiosity can sometimes get them into tight spots. Being prepared for the unexpected and knowing how to handle an emergency can mean the difference during a health crisis. At the very least, it will better equip owners to take necessary action to help their cat until a veterinarian can be contacted or medical help arrives.

It can be difficult to know when a cat is having a health crisis. Like many animals, cats may try to conceal signs of feeling unwell. In the wild, showing any kind of weakness could make a cat vulnerable to predators, so the instinct to hide feelings of sickness and injury still lingers today. In addition, cats may not exhibit key signs of emergency such as vomiting, diarrhea, or behavior changes right away. However, there are definite emergencies that will require immediate attention. Knowing what to look for and when to seek medical help is vitally important to a cat's safety. In the case of an emergency, time is of the essence. You should always be prepared for the unexpected. Being knowledgeable in the skills of first aid can save your cat's life.

It's crucial to take prompt, considered action in the case of injury or illness. However, the aim of practicing first aid treatment isn't solely about saving lives. First aid actions will provide comfort and pain relief for your cat, to aid the recovery process. By concisely listing these times, focusing on supporting subject, and providing an overall treatment plan, this section intends to give you the practical skills to be able to respond comfortably and confidently in an emergency.

CHAPTER 11

Breeding and Reproduction in Cats

The breeding of pedigree cats is a responsible and patient work that requires good training and knowledge of feline ethology as well as the standard of the breeding guidelines. In the cat fancy reproduction geopolitics should be given to choose the animals suitable for mating in line with the breeding protocols of each breed and the association references, because the breeding choices and the mating times should guide to the future proposed objectives. Responsible feline breeding begins with the responsible ownership and management of females and males dedicated to their breeding programs, starting with concern for their health, wellbeing, nutrition, and genetics.

Ethical and responsible breeding requires an understanding of the estrous cycle in female cats, menses (also called induced ovulator or reflex ovulation), mating procedure and post-mating protocols, sterilization methods, kitten management, and caring for pregnant cats. Reproductive techniques such as artificial insemination (vaginal, cervical, surgical) with fresh, chilled, or frozen semen, embryo transfer, and cryopreservation are also used. Reproductive management also includes the prevention and treatment of agents that affect the reproduction and health of cats such as hormone-related diseases, neoplasias, infertility, sexual behavior changes, and pregnancy concerns that can be concluded with cesarean sections, adoption or surgical sterilization techniques such as ovariohysterectomy or ovariectomy. In this chapter, readers will enable to better understand the breeding and reproduction of cats through detailed explanations of the estrous cycle, mating procedures, preventive solutions, birth and obstetric management, pediatric care in kittens, and behavior during pregnancy and puerperium.

CHAPTER 12

Feline Genetics and Breed-Specific Health Concerns

Although a large portion of the health issues observed in felines can now be attributed to genetic predispositions or genetics in some way, many people do not currently know much about feline genetics or the hereditary conditions that their cat may be prone to develop. Because of the misunderstanding of feline genetics' role in their health, many of these cats with possible health concerns often go undiagnosed and ignored by caretakers until they become severe health issues that require immediate intervention.

Knowing what a breed is predisposed to and what problems they commonly inherit can be an important first step for guarding your feline against such conditions. Many people consider mixed-breed pets to make better family pets since they are "genetically" not as "inbred" as many of those showing-breed felines. As a result, fewer genetic health issues are seen in cats from the local animal shelter than in those from the pedigree felines. However, these animals can still potentially fall victim to disease and disorders that are "breed-specific" owing to their mixed-breed genetics. Because cats today still have remnants of their wildcat heritage, a wild genetic predisposition may still be present in your furry friend. In this section, we cover the genetic aspects of these animals, such as the varying size and feral temperament of various breeds of cats.

In the beginning, pet felines were divided into two categories, long-haired or short-haired. It wasn't until early in the 1900s, however, when inbreeding and selective breeding came into popularity, that breeds began becoming more predictable in both personality and aesthetics. The International Cat Association now has two categories that all cat breeds are divided into, those that are based on feral foundations, and those that are based on domesticated foundations. All breeds are based on selective inbreeding, but those in the foundation, or "wild" category, are breeds in which the wild foundation bloodline is still in existence in the gene pool.

CHAPTER 13

Alternative and Complementary Therapies for Cats

The complementary therapies included in this guide are legal advancements to the Animal Welfare Act. The range of available therapies continues to grow as cats take center stage in our lives. As well, cats have become the favored companions of people in need of healing. In addition to veterinarians practicing traditional Western "conventional" medicine, there are veterinarians practicing "alternative" treatments on cats with great success. You will find alternative animal care books at many bookstores and libraries. The creation of this guide was suggested by a few of these veterinarians and is happy to do so in the interest of feline health.

In the broadest sense, complementary medicine refers to the use of therapies which serve to enhance the effectiveness of conventional veterinary medicine and the supportive care of animals. In cats, these therapies include acupuncture, massage, physical therapies such as swimming, ultrasound, laser, and proper nutrition. "Alternative" medicine, on the other hand, suggests replacing the use of traditional antibiotics or surgical procedures with an entirely different approach to healing. It is our experience that these alternative modalities are not yet part of the therapeutic picture in cats or have controversial scientific literature. These include herbal medicine, homeopathy (the use of minute doses of compounds formulated from plant, animal, and mineral sources), aromatherapy (the use of essential oils), and traditional Chinese Medicine (TCM), a complete system with a base in which surgical therapy is not included.

CHAPTER 14

The Role of Exercise and Play in Feline Health

Veterinarians emphasize the health-giving virtues of feline play. They say the same about exercise. The message is clear: exercise and play are components of a comprehensive approach to feline health. They help shed light on disease prevention and offer an accessible way to lift cats out of the sick role to which they've been consigned.

Feline activity promotes feline health. The consummate predator requires the ability to run, stalk, sprint, jump, and pounce. Exercise supplies an outlet for these needs. Games that mimic the activities of the hunt are, according to some veterinarians, "the single most important activity that housecats need for maintaining optimum health." Relatively few houses, however, are equipped with serial meadows in which cats can stretch their legs. But all cats need exercise. Without it, they gain weight and become sluggish. Lethargy leads to more inactivity, and a vicious cycle establishes itself. The result can be diabetes, liver disease, arthritis, and premature death.

Because they are hardwired for survival in the wild, cats are naturally drawn toward play that involves stalking and swiping. Given the chance, they will turn on their internal burglar alarms and creme rinse every item on their shelves to the floor. Inexpensive toys can provide outlets that are relatively easy on their humans' wallets. Besides being a way to foster health, play is also one of the few things that, once on the ground, can relieve the boredom or tension that many under-stimulated indoor cats experience. Boredom in a cat is not merely a philosophical issue. The UC Davis feline behavior specialist, Dr. Elizabeth Colleran, asks, "Do you want a bored veterinarian who plays with your cat, or a vet who is quick and efficient in seeking assistance? The exercise part of play is also a way to counter behaviors, flood the body with endorphins, and keep cats on all levels - physical, mental, and emotional - feeling good. Experts estimate that billions of play-deprived cats are coasting along on little more than a mate and their looks to see them through any given single day. They say mentally and physically stimulated cats are less likely to bite and less likely to feel stress."

CHAPTER 15

Caring for Kittens

When you bring a kitten into your home, you take on the responsibility of caring for a new life. This period of rapid growth and development is important for your kitten's future health and well-being. The following are things to consider and steps to take to ensure a growing kitten gets off to a good start. From soon after birth, kittens require mother's milk (or a suitable human baby milk replacement formulated for cats). Most of a kitten's body weight during the first few weeks of life comes from fat in milk. By the age of 5 weeks, a kitten's gastrointestinal system is mature enough to handle more complex molecules like those found in weaning and adult cat foods. When weaning kittens, you can provide them with a dish of milk replacements formulated for kittens.

In early life, kittens are developing their personalities, getting to grips with their body, and learning about their environment. It's also a very important time for their health. Most kittens are nursed by their mothers for the first 4 weeks of life. This period of nursing not only allows them to receive the benefits of their mother's nutrition-rich milk but also enables the part of the kitten's immune system that is inherited from its mother (passive immunity) time to mature. Socialization is also essential in the kitten's life. This takes place between the ages of 2 weeks and 7 weeks. The more a kitten becomes accustomed to these different elements within this period, the more easily it will integrate them into its life as an adult cat.

CHAPTER 16

Grooming and Hygiene for Cats

Cats maintain their cleanliness naturally, but you can still help them look and feel their best. Regular grooming removes excess fur, shedding hair, and dirt, reducing the amount your cat ingests and the associated hairballs. Brushing and combing also help to spread and redistribute the natural oils in your cat's skin, adding sheen and luster to her coat. Depending on the length of their hair, coat texture, and lifestyle, a cat's grooming requirements differ. Most cats will benefit from a weekly brushing, but long-haired cats may require a more comprehensive grooming routine consisting of brushing, daily combing to minimize matting, and monthly baths for optimal coat health. While cats keep themselves clean by licking their fur, it may not be sufficient to remove all of the hair or dander. You can establish a grooming routine and assist in maintaining your cat's overall cleanliness by following a few basic hygiene rules.

Body checks ensure your cat's physical health while also ensuring cleanliness, as it is possible that dirt, debris, or mats in the fur may hide an issue. Create a routine for your cat's grooming, just as you would for your skin and body care. Grooming becomes a bonding relationship as well as an acceptable routine. Encouraging an ear-to-tail wiping will allow your cat to become familiar with regular physical checks and grooming, making it easier for you to spot any changes, infections, or injuries. A weekly wipe with damp cotton wool is generally adequate to keep the eyes clean of sleep. They should be clean, bright, and free from discharge. Ensure there is no unpleasant odor emanating from their ears by examining them once a week. A gentle clean inside your cat's ear -- without pushing anything into the canal -- could be all that's required to keep it feeling comfortable and prevent wax buildup. Cats do not need to be bathed frequently since they are well-equipped to keep themselves clean. Regular grooming, on the other hand, promotes bonding and allows individuals to examine their pet in greater depth. Grooming should be enjoyable, not stressful, and should be tailored to your cat's preferences. Regular grooming aids in the development of a coat that is shiny and well-balanced and can aid in the early detection of lumps, injuries, or parasites.

CHAPTER 17

Understanding Cat Communication and Body Language

Unravel the complexities of your cat and understand what your pet is trying to communicate. Cats are complex creatures. As a society, we have bred cats that typically live in a solitary condition to now living with others. For those of us that share our homes with more than one cat, as we open the door, we hope our cats will get along. One way to ensure most cats live in harmony is to provide one or more ways for them to communicate and establish boundaries with each other. When a cat comes into contact with another of its own species, they will signal to the other cats through body language. They do much the same with people, but they also communicate with us by the noises they make.

What do cats convey with their bodies? As you share your home with your feline friend, you will notice that much of what your cat tells you is through its body language. There are many facets to a cat's body language. From where and when they arch, they are winning, eyes blinking slowly, showing tension, tail up positions, and more. Cats communicate their emotions, health, and social signals through their body language. Are you a cat whisperer? Do you feel you have a good bond with your cat? It may come as no surprise, but you are 2.5 times more likely to believe your cat communicates with you than the average person. Furthermore, 39% of cat owners feel that they have a perfect understanding of what their cat is communicating. And cats' body language does have a meaning, so spending time trying to understand it may actually make for a more pleasant interaction for you and your pet.

CHAPTER 18

The Importance of Spaying and Neutering

We must emphasize the importance of spaying and neutering and the severe consequences of not doing so. When cats reproduce, they have multiple offspring, furthering the overpopulation problem. The majority of these kittens will end up in shelters or remain on the streets. By only spaying and neutering 1 cat and preventing them from producing litters, you can eliminate the further production of tens of thousands of kittens in a matter of years. This alleviates the burden on shelters and indirectly increases the amount of time cats on the streets are kept in shelters. Furthermore, the problems of inbreeding and overpopulation contribute to high levels of poor health and can lead to kittens dying very quickly after being born.

As a final note, even if your pet cat is an indoor getaway, it may escape. If it reproduces, the number of kittens it can produce adds to the overpopulation problem. There are numerous potential locations for street cats. It's impractical to think that every kitten born on the streets will have access to a warm, healthy, stable home. Additionally, free-roaming cats can spread disease among other cats. Does spaying or neutering have any health benefits? It goes without saying that by spaying or neutering your cat, you will prevent ovarian and testicular cancers, respectively. Additionally, possibly more significantly, by avoiding reproductive cancers and eliminating the urge to mate, spaying will decrease risks connected with roaming, such as vehicle strikes, fights, and irresponsible habit compulsions. Allowing the urge for mating to persist is not a healthy way to care for your pet. Neutering can also contribute to behavioral improvements, especially in male cats.

CHAPTER 19

Traveling with Cats: Tips for a Stress-Free Journe

Traveling with cats Cats are often not keen on leaving the comforting sanctuary of their home. With a bit of preparation and a calm, gentle nature, you can make even a long trip enjoyable for your pet. We'll share some tips to help you prepare for your trip, then discuss options for getting there. Not all animals react the same way; you know your pet best and can gauge her reaction.

Before you leave, be sure to clip your pet's nails to prevent any tearing or injury when she makes an attempt to claw her way through the carrier in an attempt to escape. The following are additional suggestions to consider before taking your trip: Ensure that whatever carrier you choose is strong, well-ventilated, and large enough for your cat to stand up, turn around, and lie down in. Use either a comfortable blanket or pad that is absorbent and a little larger than the base of the carrier, so your cat can ball up on top of it. Use a leash or harness. It's always a good idea to use one when traveling, in case your pet manages to get out of the carrier. Do leave it on prior to traveling so your cat gets used to the feel of it. Make sure that your pet has a form of ID with your current contact information. Vaccinate your pet with the recommended series and consider a feline leukemia vaccine. Feed your pet a few hours before the trip and remove food after 10 hours (cats are not eating because of the car ride, they are hiding and stressed). Leave a small amount of water in the carrier. If your cat is stressed, she will not drink a lot and it may spill.

Getting there Where possible, we recommend the following four options for traveling with your cat: Trains - Although Amtrak does not currently accept pets on its trains, Greyhound does accept pets. They require not only a reasonable fare, but some advanced notice to ensure your buddy has room on board. If you take the train, you will need to purchase a carrier specifically designed to fit under the seats (a LaZ denotes carriers will not fit in compartments). Be sure to check in advance for information on requirements and limitations, prior to purchasing your tickets.

CHAPTER 20

Caring for Multiple Cats in a Household

While many cats are happy as solo felines, others thrive in multi-cat households. The dynamics of living with multiple cats can be complex, with each individual having different experiences and relationships with fellow residents. It is important to implement management strategies that will cater to the heterogeneous needs of the cats in a multi-cat household. This module reviews the behavior and welfare of multiple cats cohabiting together. We believe that one of the best ways to support the welfare of your cats is through an understanding of the social dynamics of group-living and utilizing this knowledge, along with scientifically-informed care, to provide the most supportive life possible.

Despite the complexities that can surround cats cohabiting in a group, many cats share their living spaces with at least one, or often more, fellow feline(s) with relative harmony. These cats can develop close and supportive relationships, play and groom each other, and take part in mutual activities such as allogrooming and sleeping in a group. Although group-living can come with these and other benefits, it is important to consider whether, if given free rein, a female cat would choose to cohabit in a group or live as a solitary individual. Given that cats prefer family members and have a primary and positive association with close conspecifics, it is not unreasonable to believe that many cats would choose to live with a compatible house-mate. It is also possible that some cats do not have a choice in the matter and may feel as though they are forced to cohabit in a multi-cat household. Nonetheless, most cats cohabiting together find ways to peacefully navigate shared living spaces, and owners often observe cat residents developing close and sometimes inseparable relationships.

CHAPTER 21

Cats in Different Life Stages: Kitten, Adult, and

In their lifespan, cats go through different life stages: kittens, adulthood, and senior felines. While each cat is a unique being in its own right, specializing in adapting and customizing its care plan to address whatever a cat of a certain age may encounter could be an essential component of extending the time you have with your pet and satisfying their every need.

Kittens involve a variety of care strategies, including acceptance of supervision, vaccinations, deworming, and spaying/neutering. A crucial decision-making period to ensure that they develop well and avoid any future health issues is the planning of kittens.

Adult cats require vaccinations and treatments periodically, a balanced diet, daily grooming, parasite defense, and regular veterinary visits to ensure they stay healthy and well.

Senior cats would benefit from proper veterinary maintenance and may need to pay close attention to gradual weight reduction or raise their calorie intake in reply to potential weight reduction.

Felines of various ages would need numerous amounts of nutrition. Kittens require a diet rich in minerals like calcium, proteins, and vegan vitamins for improved growth. Adult cats need stable nutrition based on the demands of the cat, including height, weight, or any underlying conditions. Adult senior cats often require a balanced diet, as most cat owners start to lose their appetite fluctuates in senior life. A weight management strategy can even be prepared through proper nutrition.

As they get older, cats face many types of health problems than when they are younger. It's a fantastic idea to provide your pet with basic treatment for senior cats, as this makes sense to track any health issues that sort of cat may experience at this age.

In caring for cats, hormones play a significant role. When we keep a tab on how the ovary works, we understand how women grow, and eventually - how they grow old - which is useful in hormone balancing therapies.

CHAPTER 22

Legal and Ethical Considerations in Feline Health

It is important for veterinary professionals to be aware of the legal and ethical framework that governs the care of cats. This includes understanding the legal requirements of what is expected of one in providing care to cats and the ethical considerations associated with providing that care. If veterinary professionals provide information about the laws or codes of practice, they should be aware that they are not qualified legal advisers and that the information provided could change due to future legislation or legal consequences.

As more culture becomes available to support responsible pet ownership, including in the appropriate care for the prevention and treatment of disease in cats, people will hopefully become more informed. This comprehensive guide is a useful resource for anyone looking for information on feline health. In particular, legal considerations associated with pet ownership are covered in Section 15, and ethical decision-making related to feline veterinary care is covered in Section 16 of this comprehensive guide to feline health care. It is important to treat cats in full accordance with the law. As a veterinary professional, it is important to know the relevant legal framework and work within that framework. Ethical decisions should be informed by the legal framework and broader ethical considerations. Using ethical best practice will ensure that all animals are considered in a welfare-friendly manner. We hope readers find the information presented in this comprehensive guide useful and informative. The sections are written by feline experts from around the world and are intended to provide a useful, informative guide to feline health care.

CHAPTER 23

Cultural and Historical Perspectives on Cats

As captivating, endearing, and beguiling as they are, cats have figured prominently in the cultural and historical frames of civilizations worldwide, even when not owned or kept by everyone. Cultural artifacts from every continent report the relationship between humans and cats going back thousands of years. Cats' physical characteristics, living habits, and relations with people have been of universal interest. In each cultural period, cats have had special roles, including gods, workers, neighbors, family members, agents of supernatural forces, symbols in religious ritual, artists' friends, objects of study, and a great variety of literature and popular expressions. Some of the reasons for a special role are based on cats' biological needs and appearances, but as an object of human knowledge, how cats have been seen is also a function of human cultural life, important in understanding social values and beliefs of different groups of people. The many ways and different reasons for which different cultural groups have represented cats reflect the immense wealth and variety in human-cat social relationships during all recorded centuries.

Researchers in the field report cats' unusual physical agility and intelligence, social life, hunting and predatory behaviors, scratching, spraying, fighting, and vocal communication. Cats' behaviors have a distinct correspondence with an attitude of independence - cats have rarely been trained or exhibited in organized animal shows. Since so many topics are possible, we confine our review and discussion to the variety of social meanings cats have had with specific links to human attitudes about cats. The present-day bond between humans and cats is not easy to decipher. Long ago, the value in eleven cultures of the ancient world was recognized. A social survey in the US showed cats' high status, and a content analysis of English children's books "based on sales and library acquisitions, found.

CHAPTER 24

The Future of Feline Health: Advances in Veterinar

New developments: Tears, lasers, Botox, and more.

There is a lot to be excited about with the future of feline health and veterinary medicine. There are new options for treating corneal sequestrums not available just a year ago. This is the result of pet owners' willingness to provide blood, the technology to concentrate healing growth factors and create a form of plasma, and the increased use of contact lenses with veterinary-eye-specialist Marcia Schwass. In her practice, Dr. Schwass also applies orthodontic braces and bridges to the mouths of cats who have had jaw fractures and have slipped their bottom canine teeth behind the top teeth. This can make surgery either to repair or to remove the teeth more expensive.

With the increasing population of cats who live indoors and higher from the street, more people are adopting cats who need medication or who have chronic feline health issues. I'd never even heard of a laser before people-vet Barrett from Houston told me that one of his cats had tears in her soft palate that were causing TMJ pain, which would require a $5,000 tooth extraction, a repair using titanium screws, and a feline dental specialist. For less than a tenth of the price, she was scheduled to visit the vet and receive a course of Botox. That is one potential treatment for cats with stomatitis or urinary idiopathic cystitis of FIC. A promising treatment is implants that appear to turn "bad" tears into normal ones. Some cats are developing genetically elongated soft palates due to trendy desired face shapes (brachycephalic syndrome) with elongated, baffling faces and airways that are increasingly twisted.

CHAPTER 25

Conclusion and Key Takeaways

The different aspects of feline health that have been detailed throughout this guide are substantial and overwhelming at times. If this section could fit at the beginning, it would be like offering readers a guide on how to build an entire car; most would suffer from information overload. But by building this guide piece by piece, you have come to follow it the whole way through and learn pieces of information and ways of thinking that you wouldn't have otherwise. The key takeaways might even have seeped into your thinking so gently that you didn't even notice it. For if you read and internalized any portion of this comprehensive guide, then you, dear reader, are one step closer to being able to offer your cat the best healthcare possible. In the wild, humans are no replacement for a cat's mother. But we can be guardians, armed with a trove of knowledge and wisdom, who can support and aid a cat throughout their entire lives. Even in those tough transition bits.

In this guide, we aimed to cover some major themes. These include everything from selecting a kitten or adopting a pregnant mother, to managing and succeeding at every life change thereafter. We provided the most up-to-date information on everything from:

- Caring for pregnant moms - Selection and preparation for homecoming with a kitten - Training - Food and nutrition - Grooming - Spaying and neutering - Environment - Preventive medicine - Vaccination - Emergencies and medical care - Lifestyle considerations.